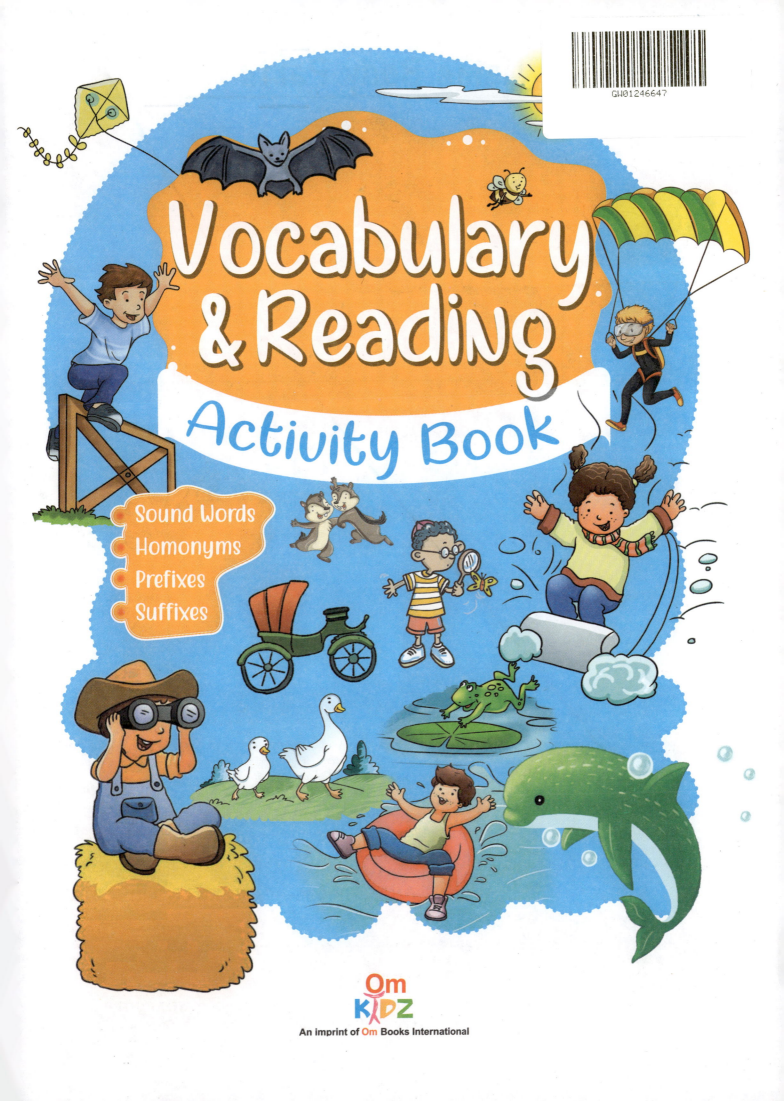

Vocabulary & Reading

Activity Book

- Sound Words
- Homonyms
- Prefixes
- Suffixes

Om KIDZ

An imprint of Om Books International

Words that Name Body Parts

2.9.23

Read the clues and fill in the crossword.

Across

1. You wear a cap on this
4. Used to eat and talk
6. This part helps you to sense sounds
7. The part of the body that gives you sight
8. Used to smell and breathe

Down

1. It is over your head and under your hat
2. Give shape to your body
3. We walk on these
5. You have it and the clock has it too–they are two in number

BONUS BOX
I have fingers and thumb but can't write. But I can keep you away from cold that's right. What am I?

Words that Name Accessories

Choose the correct word and circle it.

1. Kitty wears a bow on her
   (forehead, hand, **hair**).

2. Mr. Willie wears a belt around his
   (elbow, thigh, **waist**).

3. Mrs. Polly wears a ring on her
   (toe, **finger**, nose).

4. Lia wears a chain around her (**neck**,
   body, arm).

5. Peter wears a watch on his (hand, **wrist**, knee).

6. Ronny slings a bag over his
   (**shoulder**, back, hip).

7. Jane holds a seashell in her
   (finger, teeth, **palm**).

8. Mac takes off his shoes and
   dips his (**feet**, knees, ankles)
   into the pond.

BONUS BOX
Use the words **heads**, **shoulders**, **knees** and **toes** to make a poem of your own.
Sing it to the class.

What am I?

Tick the correct picture. Colour the letters to name the word which fits the description below.

I help the elephant splash, hold and lift things.

| B | O | X | T | R | U | N | K | I | M |

An octopus uses me to feel and grasp.

| T | E | N | T | A | C | L | E | S | O |

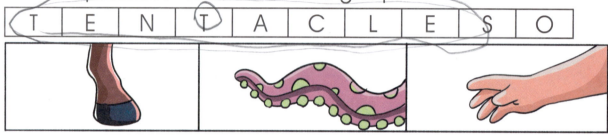

I allow fish to travel underwater.

| L | E | G | S | F | I | N | S | I | G |

A bird doesn't have teeth but I help it pick seeds

| B | E | A | K | C | L | A | W | S | X |

A tortoise hides inside me when senses danger.

| H | O | O | D | S | H | E | L | L | O |

Words that Name People

Complete the family table by circling the boxes with words that name people.

(father)	plate	pet	cat
cap	(boy)	park	home
spoon	fruits	girl	(mother)

BONUS BOX

Make your family tree and write the names of your family members. Also paste their photographs.

Words that Name Clothes

Find these clothes words in the word search.
Look across, down and diagonally.

Socks	Skirt	Coat	Pants	Jacket	Shirt	Tie	Hat

a	b	c	d	e	f	g	j	h	s
i	s	o	c	k	s	j	a	k	h
l	k	m	o	n	o	p	c	q	i
r	i	p	a	n	t	s	k	s	r
t	r	u	t	v	w	x	e	y	t
z	t	a	b	c	d	e	t	f	g
h	i	j	k	l	m	n	o	p	q
t	i	e	r	s	t	h	a	t	u

BONUS BOX

I start with an A and end with an N. I'm something you wear when you are cooking. I keep your clothes spotless. What am I?

_____ A pnun _____

Off to Work

Read the words in the word bank. Write them to match the riddle.

| teacher | dentist | policeman | fire fighter | architect | doctor |

My job is to help you when you are sick. Being fit is my trick!

__doctor__

Classroom is my place to be. You learn a lot from me

__Teacher__

I say, "Open wide" And look at your teeth inside.

__dentist__

Making plans is what I do. Building houses is my job for you.

__architect__

I help people when stuck. My tools are water, hose and truck.

__fire fighter__

I am strong and brave. My job for all is to save.

__policeman__

Words that Name Places

Help the bus reach the bus stop. Draw a line connecting all the words that name places.

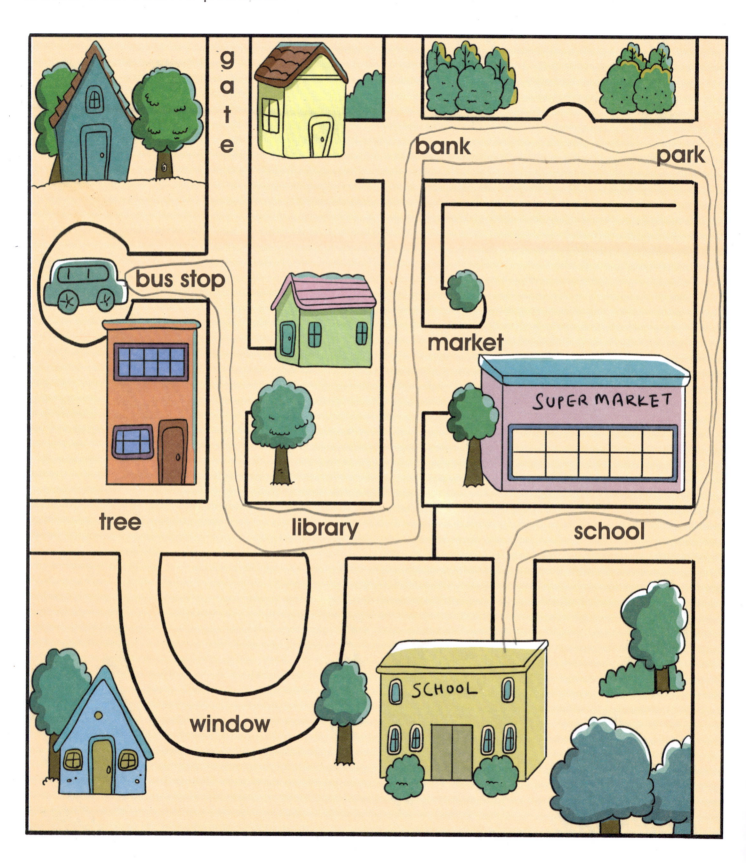

Words that Name Animals

Unscramble the words to find the names of animals that come out of the magician's hat.

1. abbrti
   rabbit

2. sanek
   snake

3. aprtro
   parot

4. abrc
   crab

5. oneymk
   monkey

6. ofrg
   frog

7. ehesp
   sheep

8. oumse
   mouse

9. urtlet
   turtlet

10. engupin
    pehguin

turtle

Were you a magician, what would you say to pop animals out of your bag? To solve the riddle, arrange the letters below in the given order.

R	A	A	B	B	R	A	D	A
1	2	3	4	5	6	7	8	9

A B R A D A B R A
2 4 1 3 8 7 5 6 9

Words that Name Things

Use the code to decode the words that name things.

A – @	B – #	C – $	D – %	E – ^	F – &	G – *	H – (	I –)
J – =	K – +	L – >	M – <	N – ?	O – "	P – }	Q – {	R – [
S –]	T – o	U – \	V – /	W – £	X – ©	Y – ÷	Z – ±	

1.
>	@	<	}
~~L~~	A	M	P

2.
#	[	\	]	(
B	R	U	S	H

3.
$	@	<	^	[	@
C	A	M	E	R	A

4.
]	"	@	}
S	O	A	P

5.
}	@	)	>
P	A	I	L

6.
$	>	"	$	+
C	L	O	C	K

7.
[	"	}	^
R	O	P	E

8.
O	)	]	]	\	^
~~T~~	I	S	S	U	E

Word Association

Draw lines to match the words that name things to the place they belong.

classroom	swing
park	bell
library	chalk
home	stamp
sky	plate
post office	book
restaurant	bed
church	kite

Use a word from above to complete each sentence.

1. Look at the little boy playing on the __Swing__.

2. Grandma gave me a story __book__.

3. Glue the __stamp__ on the postcard.

4. I can hear the __bell__ ringing.

5. Miss Lee drew a line with a __chalk__.

6. Lisa broke a __plate__ _____.

7. The lamp is beside the __bed__.

8. The __kite__ flew high in the sky.

spoon, sugar

BONUS BOX

Write names of two things with letter S you find in the kitchen.

Words that Name Fruits

Read the clues and complete the crossword puzzle.

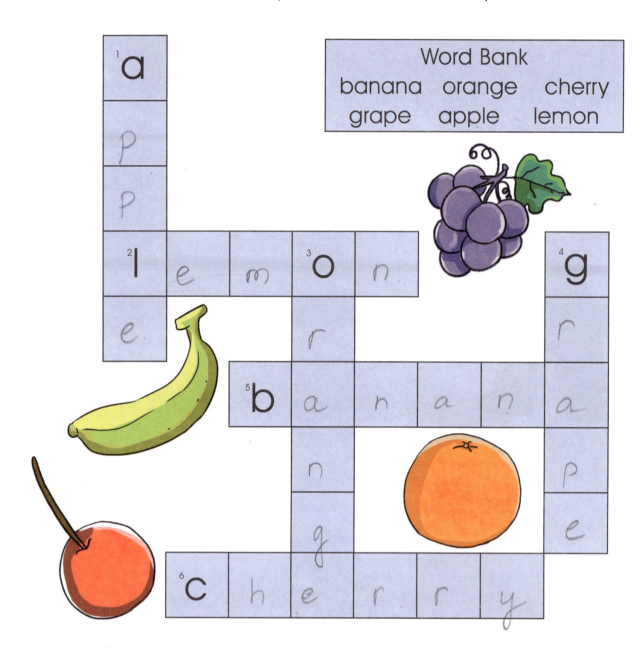

Word Bank
banana   orange   cherry
grape   apple   lemon

Across

2. I am a round, yellow fruit.
5. I am a long, yellow fruit.
6. I am red. I often hang from trees in pairs.

Down

1. I can be red, yellow or green.
3. I am the colour of a basketball.
4. I hang in bunches from vines.

BONUS BOX

I am sour and look like an orange. The word tangy comes from my name.
What am I?

29.10.24

Transport Words

The words in bold are incorrect. Correct the words with the help of each picture and write the most suitable answer above each word.

car

1. Mother drives her **boat** to the office.

2. Daddy gifted a ~~bus~~ *bike* on Mac's birthday.

3. The princess went to the ball in a ~~airplane~~ *carrige*.

4. People used to travel in ~~trucks~~ *sleigh* many years ago.

5. The men loaded the boxes into the ~~bicycle~~ *truck*.

6. We are waiting for the school ~~train~~ *Bus*.

7. The ~~ship~~ *airplane* will soon take off from the airport.

8. A ~~tram~~ *bicycle* carries a lot of people to far off places.

BONUS BOX
What is it that has three colours and controls vehicles on road?

Word Association

Cross out the word or words in each group that is not related to the words in bold.

1. Toys
top
doll
eraser
slides

2. Pets
fish
lion
rabbit
cat

3. Market
shops
grocer
ink
booth

4. Food
popcorn
jam
kettle
marble

5. School
bell
desk
classroom
mittens

6. Insects
bee
ant
butterfly
snail

7. Sports
tennis
soccer
football
stumps

8. Footwear
shoes
socks
floaters
bellies

9. Cutlery
spoon
fork
knife
mat

BONUS BOX
Choose any 4 letters from S, H, E, F, C, O and write a word that names a drink.

It's a Good Night!

Look at each picture and write what each person is saying. Use the words from the word bank below.

| Hello | Good night | Sorry | Please | Excuse me |

1. _____, may I speak to John?

2. _____ Mummy.

3. May I have some water, _____?

4. _____ Daddy.

5. _____ Miss Mary.

Action Words

Words that show an action or work are called action words.

Run, **fly** and **talk** are action words.

Read each word in the spaces below. If it is an action word, colour it green. If it is not an action word, colour it yellow.

pencil *y*

book *y*

two *y*

kick *G*

G

swim *G*

run *G*

six *y*

add *y*

a *y*

make *G*

skip *G*

flour *y*

works *y*

sleep *G*

I *y*

bed *y*

jump *G*

green *y*

talk *G*

sit *G*

she *y*

tree *y*

bird *y*

old *y*

Action Words

Complete the sentences using a word from the word box.

erases	play
read	asks
solves	counts
draws	gets

1. Jane and Kim ___plays___ a game.

2. Jane ___gets___ the board.

3. She ___draws___ a picture.

4. Jane ___asks___ Kim a riddle.

5. Kim ___read___ a book.

6. He likes to ___solve___ riddle books.

7. Jane ___counts___ to twenty.

8. Just then, Kim ___erases___ the riddle.

Play Time!

Sort these words and write them under the matching group.

jump	mew	look	run	speak	write	watch	chew
walk	neigh	chirp	draw	yell	weep	clap

eyes to see

look watch

mouth to speak

speak

hands to wave

clap draw write

legs to kick

run jump walk

animal sounds

chew yell weep chirp mew niegh

Animals in Action

What can these animals do? Tick the correct answers in the boxes given.

1. A horse can _gallop_ ☐ skip ☑ gallop

2. A cow can _moo_ ☑ moo ☐ coo

3. A parrot can _talk_ ☑ talk ☐ growl

4. A rabbit can _hop_ ☑ hop ☐ jump

5. A hamster can _squeak_ ☐ whistle ☑ squeak

6. A hen can _cluck_ ☑ cluck ☐ crow

7. A snail can _crawl_ ☐ slide ☑ crawl

8. A duck can _quack_ ☐ giggle ☑ quack

Opposites

Read each word and match the opposites.

cold

new

day

hot

night

happy

sad

little

big

old

A Cold Treat?

Use the word bank and write opposites for words below.

Word Bank:

on   far   false   win   hard   quiet   close   dirty   deep   thin

1. clean   _____

2. near   _____

3. off   _____

4. noisy   _____

5. shallow   _____

6. true   _____

7. thin   _____

8. lose   _____

9. soft   _____

10. open   _____

BONUS BOX

Write an opposite for the word **stale**. Then write a sentence with the word

On the Grill

How do these food items taste?
Choose food items and their taste and
write them in the boxes below.

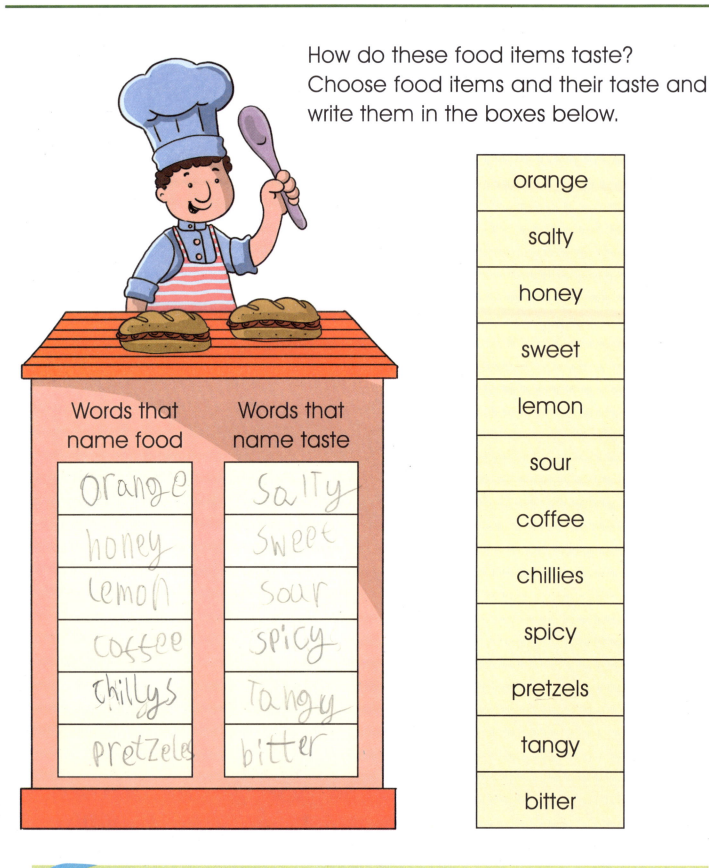

Words that name food	Words that name taste
Orange	Salty
honey	Sweet
lemon	sour
coffee	spicy
chillys	Tangy
pretzels	bitter

orange

salty

honey

sweet

lemon

sour

coffee

chillies

spicy

pretzels

tangy

bitter

BONUS BOX

Which is your favourite fruit? How does it taste?

How Does it Feel?

Match each picture to the correct word that describes how it might feel.

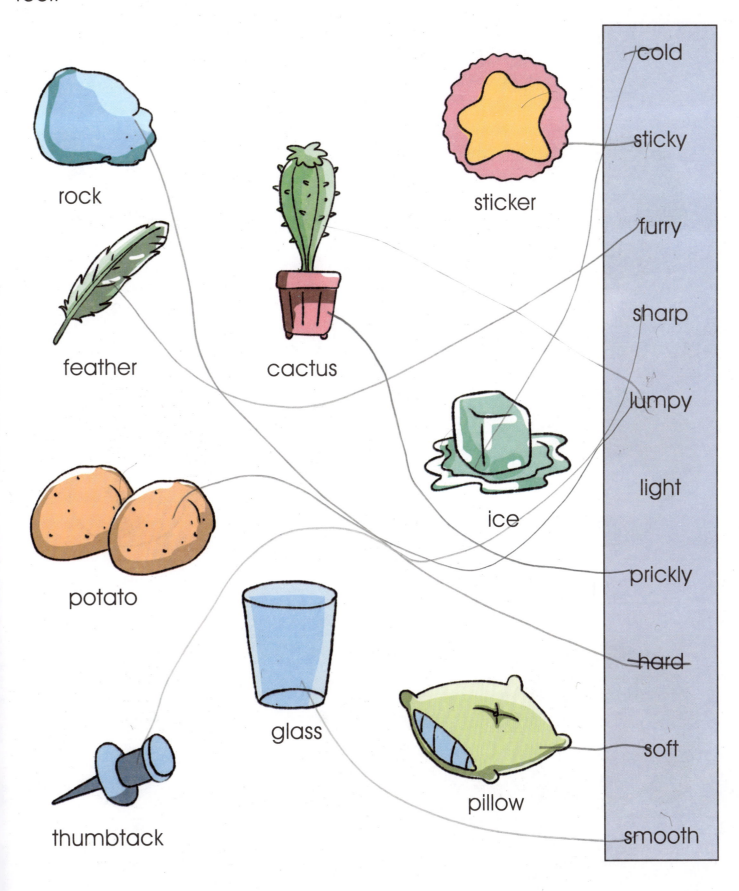

rock

feather

cactus

sticker

ice

potato

glass

pillow

thumbtack

cold

sticky

furry

sharp

lumpy

light

prickly

hard

soft

smooth

How Do You Feel?

Choose a word from the word box and write it for the matching face.

~~angry~~	~~happy~~	~~sad~~	~~worried~~	~~scared~~
~~surprised~~	~~confused~~	~~overjoyed~~	~~upset~~	

angry

happy

sad

worried

scared

suprised

confused

overjoyed

upset

Words to Describe

16d1,24.

Tick (✓) the word in each group that describes each picture.

1. tiny   hairy   fat

2. pretty   petals   stem

3. silly   funny   loving

4. pet   fast   wild

5. short   round   new

6. old   dirty   shirt

Rhyming Words

Words that sound the same at the end are called rhyming words.

For example: pair-hair, jelly-belly, ate-late

Circle the words in each group that rhyme.

BONUS BITE

Rhyming words do not have same letters at the end always. But yes they do have same sound. Like: wait–eight

1. horn   comb   corn   hen

2. tree   bee   peas   seen

3. spoon   cool   stoop   moon

4. fly   bow   tie   say

5. clock   yolk   sock   tall

6. wool   wear   full   bun

7. cloak   brown   song   down

8. ink   pluck   pick   stick

Analogies

An analogy is a comparison of two pairs of words that are related in a similar way.

For example: **bird** is to **sky** as **fish** is to **water**

Complete each analogy using a word from the word box.

1. Bus is to road as boat is to ___Sea Sea___. *S SS*

2. Stars are to night as sun is to ___day___ .

3. Straw is to drink as spoon is to ___Scooping___ .

4. Cap is to head as shoes is to ___feet___ .

5. Blue is to sky as red is to ___apple___ .

6. King is to man as queen is to ___lady___ .

7. Toe is to foot as finger is to ___hand___ .

8. Grapes is to fruit as peas is to ___vegatables___ .

BONUS BOX

Make your own pairs of analogies and quiz your friends.
Write any two pairs here.

Words Often Confused

Tick the correct answers in the boxes below.

1. Carol wore a __pair__ of bellies to the party.

   [✓] pair   [ ] pear

2. The baby slept with the teddy __bear__.

   [ ] bare   [✓] bear

3. Jack climbed up a __bean__ stalk.

   [ ] been   [✓] bean

4. The glass of milk is __too__ sweet to drink.

   [ ] two   [✓] too

5. __one__ of the chairs is broken.

   [ ] won   [ ] one

6. I don't think __it__ will rain today.

   [✓] it   [ ] eat

7. They have forgot __their__ books here.

   [ ] there   [✓] their

8. __Wait__ till the rain stops.

   [ ] weight   [✓] wait

Who's the Winner?

Play this game with your friends and help the children reach the school.

Start

What do you write with?	Where do you wear a backpack?	What do we use to cut cloth?

 peh

 back

 sissors

What do you use to stick things?

 Glue

Which game is this?	Who do you see when you are sick?	What days do you go to school?	What takes you to school?

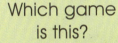 football

 docter

week day

Monday Tuesday Weansday

BUS

What tells us the time? clock

What do you sit on?

Chair

Where do you find books and read quietly?

 l'ibary

Finish

Alphabetical Order

Alphabetical order is a way to sort a list. It is done by following the usual order of letters in an **alphabet**.

bus, engine, airplane, helicopter, car

↓

airplane, bus, car, engine, helicopter

Alphabetical order makes it easier to find a name or a title in the list.

Rewrite each word list in ABC order

hop, top, pop, mop

grass, flower, bench, tree

shoes, jacket, trousers, cap

cupcake, pastry, bread

1. hop mop pop top

2. bench flower grass tree

3. cap jacket shoes trousers

4. bread cupcake pastry

Alphabetical Order

Find the words in the word search below. Then write the words in the alphabetical order.

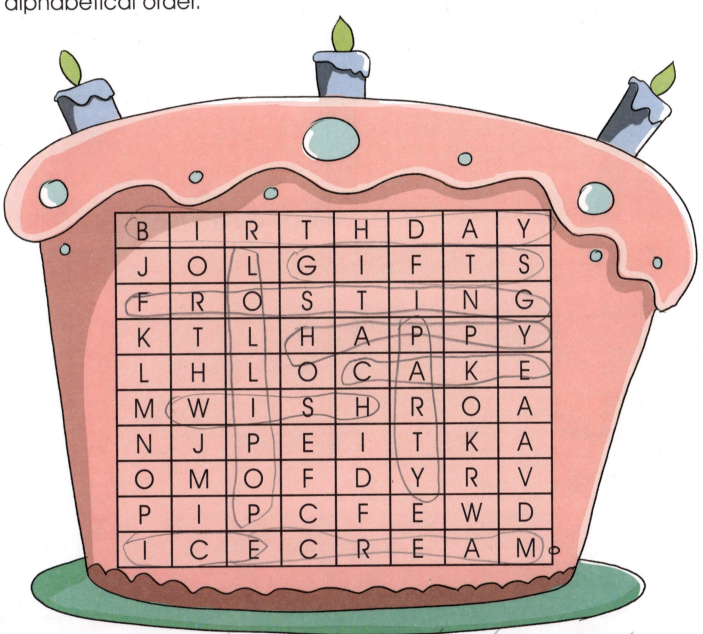

B	I	R	T	H	D	A	Y
J	O	L	G	I	F	T	S
F	R	O	S	T	I	N	G
K	T	L	H	A	P	P	Y
L	H	L	O	C	A	K	E
M	W	I	S	H	R	O	A
N	J	P	E	I	T	K	A
O	M	O	F	D	Y	R	V
P	I	P	C	F	E	W	D
I	C	E	C	R	E	A	M

happy birthday wish ice cream cake gifts frosting lollipop party

1. _birthday_

2. _cake_

3. _frosting_

4. _gifts_

5. _happy_

6. _icecream_

7. _lollipop_

8. _party_

9. _wish_

Sorting Words

Write the words under the right categories.

Food

Drink

pasta	milk	eggs	tea	cornflakes
patty	coffee	cheese	water	toast
noodles	almonds	butter	kiwi	bread

TRY IT! In which list will you add ice?

Sort the Words into Different Categories

Read the words and sort them according to their categories. Write them under the right categories.

eyebrows, short, market, shoes, tall, grandmother, nose, bank, zoo, jacket, cheeks, long, airport, big, lips, aunt, gloves, daughter, trousers, mother

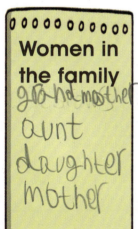

Women in the family
grandmother
aunt
daughter
mother

Places
market
bank zoo
airport

Things you wear
shoes
jacket
gloves
trousers

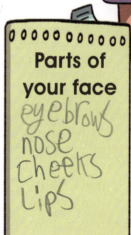

Parts of your face
eyebrows
nose
cheeks
lips

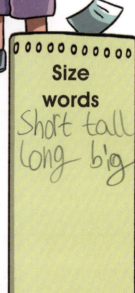

Size words
short tall
long big

 TRY IT! Add one word of your choice each to the list on this page.

Words That Go Together

In each tile, colour three words that go together. Find the words across, down and even diagonally.

book	rain	light
cars	magazine	sun
clock	chair	newspaper

bird	goat	squirrel
grass	ladybug	orange
pillow	quilt	blanket

vast	sick	squid
huge	happy	octopus
giant	healthy	drawers

drill	grandma	cucumber
square	eggplant	sea
spinach	wise	sleep

sky	cookies	twelve
woods	mountain	forest
sausage	tomato	trousers

lake	pond	stream
indigo	pink	poppy
bark	branch	nest

Odd One Out

In each group, find the word that is not like the others. Circle it.

1. pills, doctor, hospital, secretary, nurse

2. aunt, sister, mother, uncle, niece

3. shoe, skirt, shirt, suit, smart

4. Thursday, November, December, May, April

5. good, nice, friendly, kind, tawny

6. beak, wings, ducklings, claws, feathers

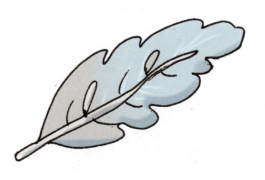

Words with Related Meanings

Put a (✔) on the correct word.

1. Which two words name things you drink from?

   glass   cup   plate

2. Which two words name things you do with your eyes?

   watch   see   tell

3. Which two words name things you do with money?

   pay   sell   buy

4. Which two words name ways to make art?

   draw   paint   cut

5. Which two words tell you that something is not old?

   young   ancient   new

6. Which two words tell you how sure you are?

   know   guess   sure

7. Which two words name bad feelings?

   cross   jolly   angry

Difference Between Related Words

Circle the correct option for each question below.

1. Which one of these is inside?

   the ground   (the floor)

2. Which belongs to you?

   (a pet)   an animal

3. Which is faster?

   stroll   (run)

4. Which of these is younger?

   (calf)   cow

5. Which is bigger?

   a jump   (a leap)

6. Which is more sudden?

   (pulling)   (yanking)

7. Which is stronger?

   (a wind)   a breeze

8. Which is later?

   in the evening   (at night)

Synonyms

A synonym is a word that has nearly the same meaning as another word.

For example: tiny-wee

Match the words to their synonyms.

1. cry

2. silent

3. warm

4. far

5. difficult

6. start

7. alone

8. true

9. quick

10. rich

hot

hard

fast

weep

correct

wealthy

quiet

begin

lonely

distant

Synonyms

Choose the correct word and write the synonym for the words given below.

| large | yell | noisy | sugary | gift | talk |

speak _____

big _____

present _____

shout _____

loud _____

sweet _____

Synonyms

Using the across and down clues, write the matching words in the cross-word below.

Across

4. commented
5. loaf
8. rock
9. shortly

Down

1 task
2 donate
3 record
6 grade
7 rush
8 stain

a. list   b. chores   c. rank   d. give   e. spot
f. bread   g. stone   h. soon   i. dash   j. said

Antonyms

An antonym is a word that is opposite in meaning to another word.
For example: **new-old**

Choose the word that has the opposite meaning of the first word in each set.

1. quiet   noisy   silent

2. tidiness   clean   mess

3. loose   tight   fixed

4. shallow   wet   deep

5. deny   take   accept

6. none   every   zero

7. shrink   narrow   grow

8. polite   rude   generous

 TRY IT! Write as many antonyms as you can for the word, big. How many did you find?

Antonyms

Choose the best antonym for the following words and show Kate the way to reach the cottage and hide.

break
seek
weak
win
remove
leave
exit

Hide

Reach

Enter

Lose

Strong

Repair

Add

Antonyms

foolish   difficult

sour   lost

never   new

disagreed   dislike

common   found

Write the antonym of the underlined words.

1. I have <u>found</u> my favourite toy.

    _____

2. The test was <u>easy</u> for me.

    _____

3. Jane <u>always</u> does her work on time.

    _____

4. Mother <u>likes</u> some hot water with lemon.

    _____

5. Roger's team <u>won</u> the soccer match.

    _____

6. The farmer picked some <u>sweet</u> apples from the orchard.

    _____

7. We all <u>agreed</u> with our new captain.

    _____

8. The teacher showed us picture of <u>rare</u> animals.

    _____

9. Eddie was <u>wise</u> to jump into the cool pool.

    _____

10. Let us decorate the class with <u>old</u> ribbons.

    _____

Compound Words

A compound word is a word made of two or more words used together. For example: shoe + lace= shoelace

Read each word below. Combine it with a word from the help box and form a compound word.

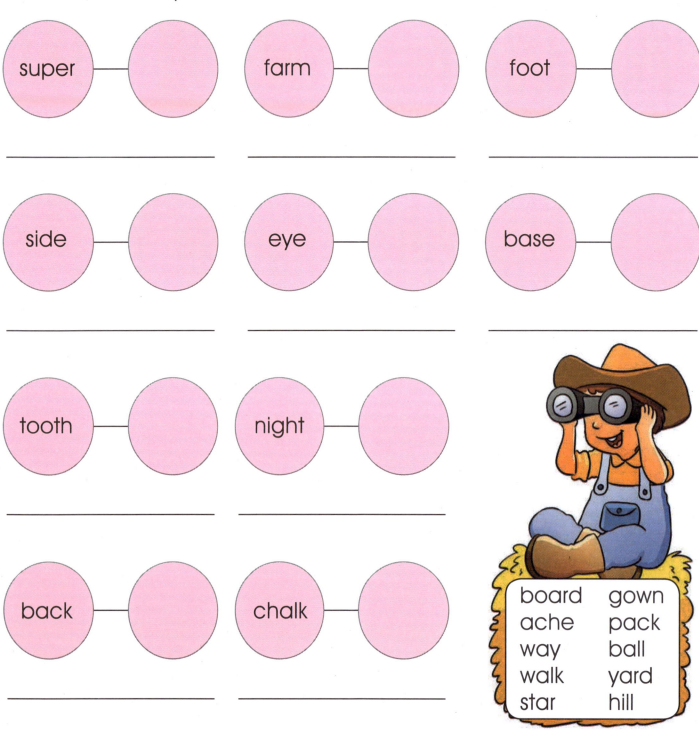

super ⬡—⬡

_____

farm ⬡—⬡

_____

foot ⬡—⬡

_____

side ⬡—⬡

_____

eye ⬡—⬡

_____

base ⬡—⬡

_____

tooth ⬡—⬡

_____

night ⬡—⬡

_____

back ⬡—⬡

_____

chalk ⬡—⬡

_____

board	gown
ache	pack
way	ball
walk	yard
star	hill

Compound Words

Write compound words using the help box given here.

help box

team	score	town	shield
sun	work	sick	pole
wind	track	self	drum
		keeper	set
		my	stick
		down	flag
		home	race

1. _____

2. _____

3. _____

4. _____

5. _____

6. _____

7. _____

8. _____

9. _____

10. _____

11. _____

12. _____

TRY IT Add ship, board and ball to words of your choice and make compound words.

Using Compound Words in Context

Draw lines to make compound words. Use the new words in the sentences given below.

1. _____ is a nice winter day.

2. The _____ is bright and warm.

3. John slides down the _____ past the car.

4. He turns around at the _____.

5. He and his sister Olive play in the snow and make _____.

6. Olive wants to make a _____ too.

7. John runs into the house to get _____ he collected last summer.

8. They make a big snowman and decorate it with the _____ John brought.

sun	man
to	shells
snow	shine
side	way
drive	balls
snow	thing
some	day
sea	walk

Using Compound Words

Circle the pair of words that make a compound words. Then fill in the blanks using an appropriate compound word.

break	way	through	fast
pan	cakes	walk	over
door	knob	bell	side
sun	ray	due	shine
door	knob	way	bell
table	cloth	land	chair
tea	pot	berry	spoon
sun	bun	back	flowers

Nora was preparing_____. Just as she began

heating up the frying pan for _____, the _____

rang. She took the frying pan off the stove and

went to answer the door. As she opened the door,

_____ spilled in through the _____.

"Welcome I'm glad you could come by for breakfast.

Come in and have a seat, Abby." she said.

Nora spread a _____ on the table and set out her

crystal _____ beside the vase of _____.

Nora and Abby sat down and had a

delicious breakfast together.

Prefix and Suffix

Prefix

A prefix is a word part placed at the beginning of a word. It changes the meaning of a word.

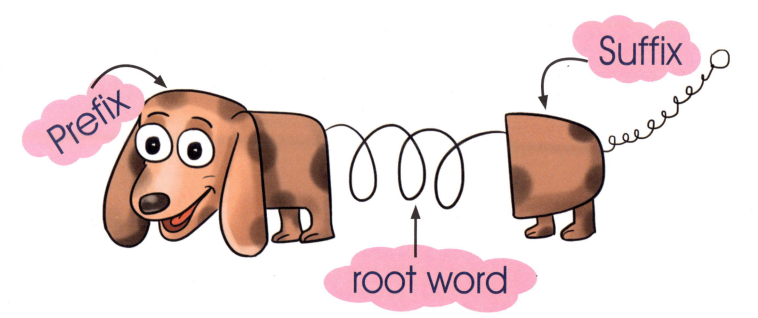

Read the common prefixes, their meanings and and words as examples.

dis		dishonest - not honest
un		unhappy - not happy
mis	NOT	misplaced - not in right place
im		improper - not proper
in		inactive - not active
re	do again	refill - fill again
pre	before	premade - made before
de	from	derail - go from the rail
bi	two	bisect - separated into two

Prefixes

Choose and add a suitable prefix to the given words to make new words.

_____ stop

_____ fund   _____ test

_____ fair   _____ behave

_____ like   _____ real

_____ play   _____ turn

Dis
Non
Re
Un
Pre
Mis
Bi

Prefixes

Add one of the prefixes to the words and complete the sentences.

un	re	pre	mis	dis

1. Grandma told me to wait till my birthday to _____ **wrap** the gifts.

2. The baker had to _____ **heat** the oven before he could put the cookies in.

3. Linda forgot her backpack and had to _____ **turn** home to get it.

4. Ashley was sad because she was _____ **able** to get tickets for the magic show.

5. I was about to fall as my shoelaces were _____ **tied**.

6. Imme had to _____ **do** the math problems.

7. Be careful not to _____ **spell** the words on the poster.

8. Sharon was being _____ **honest** when she did not tell the truth.

Prefixes

A prefix is a word part added at the beginning of a base word to change the meaning of that word.

Example: re + write = rewrite (to write again)

Tick each box with a correct definition

rewrite write again	**unkind** not kind	**preschool** before school	**bicycle** one-wheeled vehicle
midnight in the middle of night 12:00	**dislike** like very much	**unsolved** not solved	**improper** perfect
non-stop without stopping	**overeat** eat too much	**subway** under a road	**replace** place something again
inactive not active	**exhale** breathe out	**invisible** clearly seen	**cooperate** work jointly

Prefixes

Fill in the blanks by adding a prefix to the words in brackets. Then write the number that matches the meaning of the word.

1. Abbie loves to do pottery. She always _____ (plans) her projects.

2. She does not like _____ (order).

3. First she _____ her tools (arranges).

4. Then Abbie brings in an _____ lump of clay (formed).

5. She slowly _____ the lump (shapes).

6. Abbie is _____ to see that the lump doesn't take a proper shape (happy).

7. She _____ upon her idea (thinks).

8. She _____ the project and moves the wheel carefully this time (starts).

9. The lump _____ and comes to shape a big pot! (appears)

10. Abbie paints the pot and puts it on a _____ (view).

_____ opposite of appears	_____ shapes again	___ sad	___ think again
___ plan before	__ not formed	____ not in order	____ show in advance
	___ start again	___ arrange before	

Suffixes

A suffix is a word part placed at the end of a word. It changes the meaning of a word.

Here are some common suffixes, their meaning and an example.

Suffix	Meaning	Example
-ful	full of	hopeful
-ist	person who is	artist
-ly	in a way	slowly
-ion	act of/ condition of being	protection
-less	without	helpless
-ible	can be	collectible
-ness	being	sickness
-able	can be	washable
-er/-or	one who	trainer/protector
-ish	having the quality of	childish
-dom	place or state of being	freedom

More Suffixes

Pick and add a suffix to each root word to make new words.

1. most   –   _____
2. beauty –   _____
3. tour   –   _____
4. cold   –   _____
5. move   –   _____
6. late   –   _____
7. drive   –   _____

-ful
-ist
-ly
-ment
-er
-est
-able

Circle the word that contains a suffix in each sentence below.

1. The team was hopeful to win the match.

2. The students of our class have a lot of unity.

3. Sam was very careless when running in the rain.

4. If you don't eat proper food, it will cause weakness.

5. Please don't throw that bag. It can be useful.

6. Mom bought a new gift for me that is portable.

7. The sunrise we saw over the mountains was really beautiful.

8. The warmest time of the year is best for growing these plants.

9. Many plants become droopy if you don't water them well.

10. The old man had a lot of wisdom.

Squirrels Serving

Use a prefix or suffix from the list to form a word for each meaning. Write each word in the puzzle.

1. write again
2. read wrongly
3. without care
4. able to agree
5. being kind
6. opposite of appear
7. use wrongly
8. not covered
9. state of being sick
10. opposite of honest
11. not fair
12. full of help

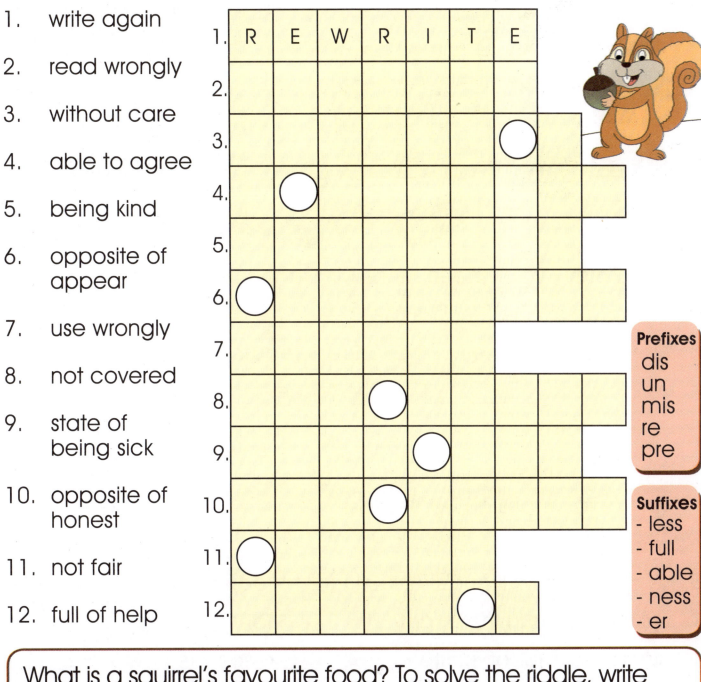

1. R E W R I T E

Prefixes
dis
un
mis
re
pre

Suffixes
- less
- full
- able
- ness
- er

What is a squirrel's favourite food? To solve the riddle, write each circled letter from above on the matching number below.

_____ _____ _____ _____ _____ _____ _____ _____ _____
 7   11   18   5   15   12   17   1   3

Suffixes

Complete the sentences by adding a suffix to the words in bold.

A suffix is a word that is added at the end of a word to change the meaning of that word.

1. Some **play**_____ sheep broke Mr. Franc's fence.

2. He wonders if the fence is **use**_____.

3. Mr. Franc thinks whether the fence is **repair**_____.

4. He looks **sad**_____ at the fence.

5. He **immediate** _____ calls his friend Mr John.

6. Mr. John is a **skil** _____ handyman.

7. He repairs fences and gates **fast**_____ than other handymen.

8. He comes to Mr Franc's farm with all his **equip**_____.

9. Mr. John works in the **bright**_____ of the day.

10. Mr. Franc is full of **excite** _____ to see the new fence.

Hints   -ful -ly -ment -able -er -ness

Suffixes

Complete each sentence by adding a suffix to the base word.

1. Toby and Abby took a rest_____ night's sleep before hiking.
2. They packed their backpacks and did not carry anything break_____.
3. Abby wore comfort_____ shoes.
4. Toby's shoes are sturdy and wear_____.
5. The children also carry a jacket in case the day is cold and wind_____.
6. The group was full of excite_____.
7. Toby was the lead____ of the group.
8. He told the group not to litter and keep the trails spot_____.
9. The children are thought_____ and help each other while hiking.
10. They speak softly because loud_____ sounds can scare animals.
11. Everyone was happy to see colour_____ flowers and animals.
12. The trip was memor_____ for the children.

Using Suffixes

Fill in the crossword by adding a suffix to the words in the word bank. Read the hints for changing spellings.

Across

3. state of being dense

6. full of courage

8. one who is slow than the other

10. the act of celebrating

Down

1. a person who makes art

2. without fear

4. state of being perfect

5. something that can be solved   7. something that can be read

9. full of help

Quick tip!

We add or remove letters while adding suffixes to some words. For example: to add –ion to celebrate, drop the e at the end and add –ion. The new word is celebration.

Word bank

solve

help

perfect

courage

dense

fear

celebrate

slow

art

read

-ion or –tion: action or process

-ity: state of being

-ment: action or process

-able: can be done

-less: without

-ous: full of

-er: more

Homophones

SAME sounds

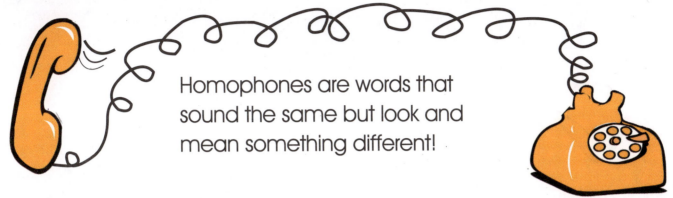

Homophones are words that sound the same but look and mean something different!

Let us read some examples.

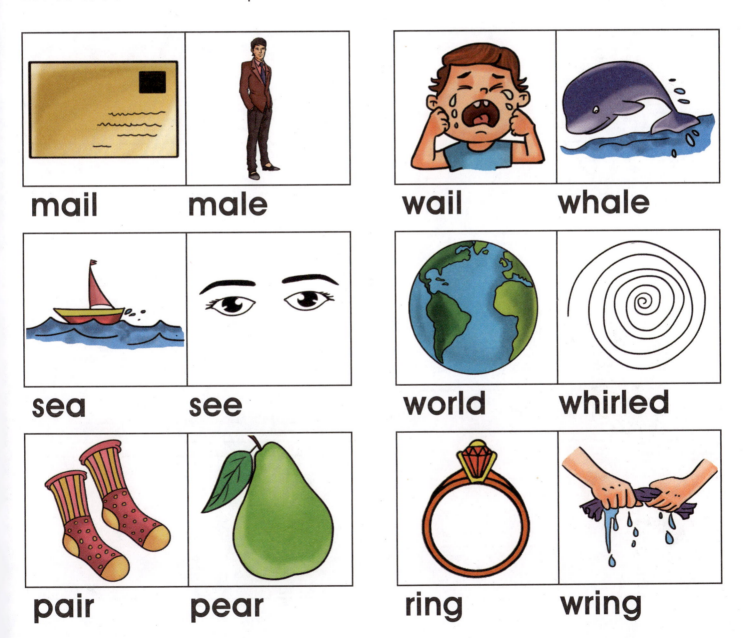

mail   male

wail   whale

sea   see

world   whirled

pair   pear

ring   wring

Drawing Homophones

Look at the picture and write a word for it. Now write its homophone and draw its picture.

<u>Right</u>

_____

_____

_____

_____

Writing Homophones

Write a homophone for each word given below.

1. be   –   _____

2. break   –   _____

3. i   –   _____

4. knot   –   _____

5. main   –   _____

6. ate   –   _____

7. dew   –   _____

8. no   –   _____

9. blew   –   _____

10. hair   –   _____

11. week   –   _____

12. some   –   _____

13. roll   –   _____

14. pain   –   _____

15. right   –   _____

 TRY IT! Think of two homophones of the word sent. Then write sentences to show the difference between the three words.

Writing Correct Homophones

Choose the correct word to complete the sentence.

1. Last Monday, I _____ (road, rode) a pony along the trail in the mountains.

2. My dog hurt its _____ (paws, pause) from digging in the yard.

3. My sister _____ (passed, past) her time by reading stories.

4. My father cut the _____ (bored, board) in half to build a tree house.

5. We _____ (one, won) all the matches this year.

Make sentences with these pairs of homophones.
1. scene - seen
_____
_____

2. tail - tale
_____
_____

3. stair - stare
_____
_____

Homographs

Homographs are words that share the same spelling, regardless of how they are pronounced. Let us read some homographs.

bat

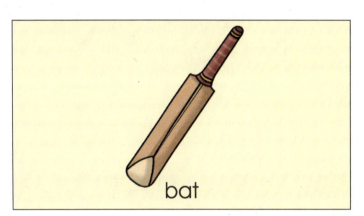

bat

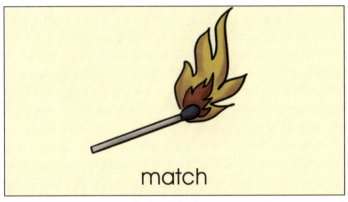

match

match

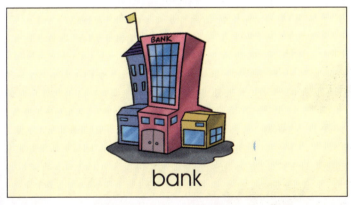

bank

bank

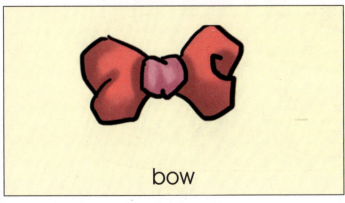

bow

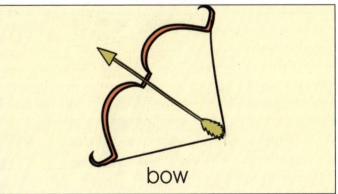

bow

Homographs

Use each word given below in sentences to show two different meanings it has. One has been done for you.

1.　park - Dad parks his car in the garage.
　　The children are playing in the park.

2.　saw - _____
　　_____

3.　tie - _____
　　_____

4.　watch - _____
　　_____

5.　row - _____
　　_____

Making New Words

Use letters in each word below to build some four-letter words. The rule is not to change the order of the letters as they occur in the word. You may skip over some letters and move backward and forward.

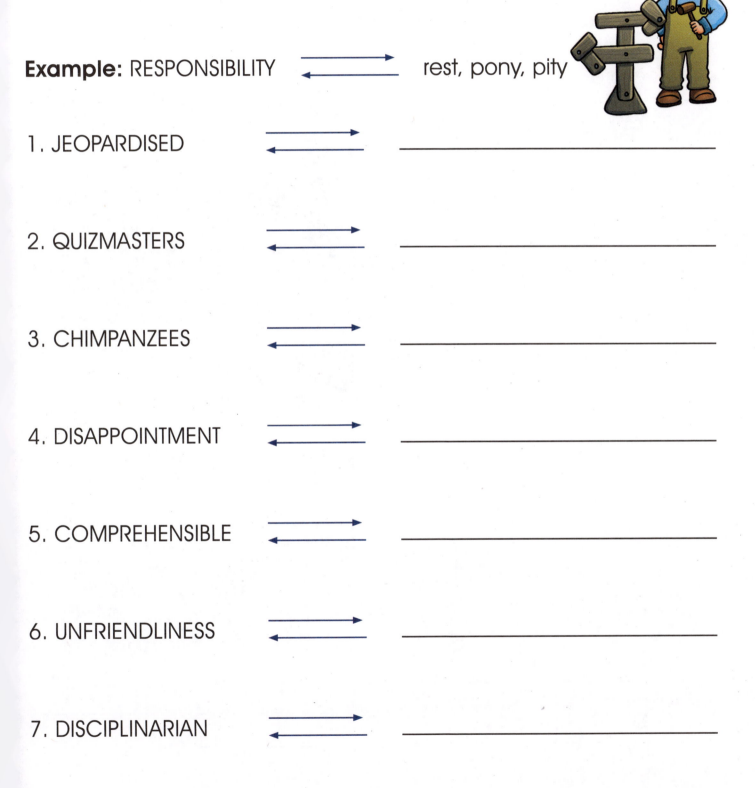

Example: RESPONSIBILITY   ⟶⟵   rest, pony, pity

1. JEOPARDISED   ⟶⟵   _____

2. QUIZMASTERS   ⟶⟵   _____

3. CHIMPANZEES   ⟶⟵   _____

4. DISAPPOINTMENT   ⟶⟵   _____

5. COMPREHENSIBLE   ⟶⟵   _____

6. UNFRIENDLINESS   ⟶⟵   _____

7. DISCIPLINARIAN   ⟶⟵   _____

Anagrams

An anagram is a word or phrase made by rearranging the letters of another word or phrase.

Example: spot-pots, post, stop

Rearrange the letters in each word below and write an anagram in the space provided.

| S | T | A | R |
| | | | |

| V | E | I | L |
| | | | |

| W | A | R | D |
| | | | |

| D | I | S | K |
| | | | |

| F | A | C | E |
| | | | |

| G | U | L | P |
| | | | |

| R | O | S | E |
| | | | |

What happened when four couples went to a restaurant?

Rearrange the letters to form the surprise answer.

| I | G | E | H | T | T | A | E |
| | | | | | | | |

Root Words

A root word is the basic word that exists in a language. It has no added letters. We can add letters to root words to make other words and change their meaning.

Look at the words on each cap. Colour the cap if the word is a root word.

Root Words

Identify the root word of the words in the word bank. Complete each sentence using the root words.

Word bank

replay	lovely
enjoyable	rebuild
nicely	coldness
sleepy	ending
preheat	retry

1. Lee and his friends like to _____ in the snow.

2. They _____ sledding down the hill.

3. Ronny and Kate may have a _____ snow fight.

4. They _____ to make big balls of snow.

5. All the children are covered with snow by the _____.

6. Lee's friends also _____ to make an igloo.

7. They _____ high walls!

8. Soon it grew _____ outside.

9. The children go home to _____ some cocoa.

10. Then everyone is ready to go to _____

Inflectional Endings

Inflectional endings are letters added to the end of a word that change its meaning. **-s, -ed, -ing, -er, -est** are inflectional endings.

Example: play- plays, played, playing

Write each new word on the line. Follow the spelling rules.

1. dive + ed = _____

2. carry + ed= _____

3. talk + ed = _____

4. wash + ed = _____

5. skip + ed = _____

6. try + ed = _____

7. plan + ed = _____

8. jog + ed = _____

9. hurry + ed = _____

10. hop + ed = _____

Spelling rules
1. If a word ends with a short vowel and one consonant, double the consonant. Then add – *ed* or –*ing*.
2. If a word ends with e, drop the e and then add – *ed or –ing*.
3. If a word ends with y, change the y to *i*. Then add –*ed*.

Inflectional Endings

Read the words in the word bank.
Add –ed, -ing, or -s and then write the
word in the correct group.

Word bank

~~flap~~	hope	~~plan~~
~~lift~~	~~fit~~	~~grab~~
~~cook~~	~~sting~~	drag
skip	jump	~~crawl~~
~~save~~	~~walk~~	melt

Add -s

flaps   plans

grabs drags

fits   stings

skips crawls

melts

Add -ed

flaped hoped

liftneed fitted

grabed cooked

saved draged

walked melted

Add -ing

planing sitting

draging crawling

jumping skiping

Greek Roots

We use some Greek roots to form new words in English. Read the list of some Greek roots in the table given below.

TRY IT Use any 5 Greek roots and make 3 words for each.

Greek Root	Meaning	Greek Root	Meaning
aero	air	meter	measure
anthr	main	mono	one
ast	star	onym	name
biblio	book	opt	eye
bio	life	ortho	straight
cardi	heart	path	feeling
chrom	colour	phil	love
chron	time	phob	fear
cycl	circle	phon	sound
derm	skin	photo	light
geo	earth	phys	nature
gon	angle	phyte	plant
graph	write	pod	foot
hydr	water	scop	see
log	word	therm	heat

Greek Roots

Circle the Greek roots in each word below. Then write the letter of its meaning on the blank.

a. telephone
b. autograph
c. bicycle

d. phonics
e. hemisphere
f. biology

g. monogram
h. hydrosphere
i. thermometer

Now use the roots from the above words to complete these words.

1. _____ ical
2. _____ al
3. _____ scope

4. _____ mobile
5. _____ sphere
6. sym_____ ny

7. _____ lone
8. _____ ant
9. _____ logue

word bank

_____ far
_____ sound
_____ water
_____ half
_____ one
_____ two
_____ life
_____ heat
_____ by itself

Contractions

A contraction is a short form of a word or words. These are formed by replacing missing letters with an apostrophe.

For example: he will – he'll

Use the words on each gift to make contractions. Write them on the blanks.

7. _____

1. _____   4. _____

8. _____

2. _____   5. _____

9. _____

3. _____   6. _____   10. _____

Contractions

Read the sentences.
Replace the underlined words by a contraction.

1. <u>It is</u> Christmas today.
2. <u>We are</u> looking for Martha's present.
3. <u>Where is</u> the present kept?
4. Jacob thinks <u>it is</u> behind the wardrobe.
5. <u>I am</u> going to look for the present in the living room.
6. Tina <u>does not</u> remember seeing Martha's present.
7. Jacob and Martha also said they <u>had not</u> seen her present.
8. <u>They have</u> been searching all around the house.
9. <u>I will</u> look for the present in the garage.
10. Martha <u>cannot</u> wait until the celebration begins.

Quick Tip! We use **'s** to show contractions and possessive nouns. **It's** is the contraction of **It is**. **Martha's** means something that belongs to Martha.

Contractions

Fill in the blanks with suitable contractions from the given options and read the sentences..

1. Poor Maria _____ invited to the party.
2. Her friends are invited. They _____ wait to go there.
3. _____ been planning for it all day.
4. Maria _____ feel happy about it.
5. She _____ have a nice dress to wear at the party
6. Maria's sister _____ allow her to go anyway.
7. _____ stay at home by herself.
8. Maria thinks _____ unfair that she has not been invited.
9. But _____ a surprise waiting for her!
10. Her friends _____ believe it when they see the surprise.

doesn't, it's, isn't,
they've, wouldn't,
there's, didn't,
hasn't, she's, she'll,
can't, won't

Fun With Words

Here's a crazy puzzle! Add letter z to each word below. You can add the letter in the beginning, middle or at the end. Then rearrange the words to make a new word.

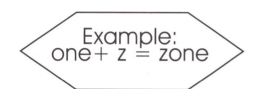

Example:
one + z = zone

1. spa + z = _____

2. ill + z = _____

3. bear + z = _____

4. are + z = _____

5. ero + z = _____

6. ame + z = _____

7. doe + z = _____

8. moo + z = _____

9. ripe + z = _____

10. roar + z = _____

11. done + z = _____

12. noose + z = _____

TRY IT

What does an alarm do continuously to wake you up?
Hint: It has a z in it!

Silent Letters

Silent letters are letters of a word that you can't hear when you say it. Example: knew is pronounced as new as the k is silent.

Identify the silent letter or letters in each word below and circle it.

1. Calm
2. Hour
3. Knot
4. Folk
5. Walk
6. Knee
7. Gnaw
8. Tomb
9. Choir
10. Doubt

TRY IT Say this tongue-twister 5 times quickly and identify the words that have a silent letter?
John Johnson joined Jenny Jerry in eating whole apple jelly.

Silent Letters

Unscramble the letters to complete each sentence with silent-letter words.

1. Suzie's holidays are _____ (htrig) around the corner.

2. She has only _____ (ghtie) days left for shopping.

3. Suzie _____ (houtght) about all that she wants to buy.

4. She and her mother _____ (rwote) a list.

5. They went shopping an _____ (uhro) later.

6. Suzie _____ (ghtbou) a cap for her sister.

7. She bought a warm _____ (niktedt) scarf for her mother.

8. She _____ (rawppde) her presents nicely.

TRY IT Write 3 words each with silent k and w. Circle the silent letters.

Word Choices

Word choice refers to the selection of words to make your writing interesting.
Example: I heard a mew and went into the room.
I heard a mew and rushed into the room.

Choose the best word for each sentence given below.

1. James _____ his swimsuit out of the drawer.
   a. got | b. yanked

2. He _____ his swim tube from under the bed.
   a. looked | b. spotted

3. James _____ on his water goggles.
   a. grabbed | b. put

4. Then he _____ out of the room.
   a. went | b. dashed

5. The pool water was _____ with chlorine.
   a. cleaned | b. disinfected

6. James _____ into the pool and enjoyed himself.
   a. jumped | b. splashed

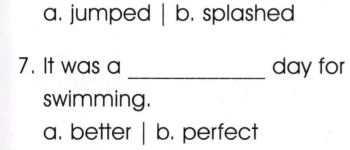

7. It was a _____ day for swimming.
   a. better | b. perfect

Word Skills

Use the codes below to write the opposite of each word.

1. always
— — — — —
8 % / % *

2. strong
— — — —
= % @ 5

3. sweet
— — — —
& 9) *

4. shallow
— — — —
& % % ?

5. idle
— — — —
) & :

6. agree
— — — — — — — —
& 3 & @ 1 * % %

7. rare
— — — — — —
$ 9 7 7 9 8

8. rapid
— — — —
& 6 9 =

9. full
— — — — —
% 7 ? (:

10. danger
— — — —
& @ > %

code

a- @   b- #   c- $
d- &   e- %   f- >
g- 1   h- 2   i- 3
j- 4   k- 5   l- 6
m- 7   n- 8   o- 9
p- ?   q- +   r- *
s- &   t- (u-)
v- /   w- =   x- <
y- :   z- [

Words Often Confused

Choose the correct options and complete the sentences. Find the words in the puzzle.

```
N O X M H R Y R L B
P U Y F A I R I I Y
I U T H E R E G M V
E A R B A D N H K I
C T H E R E H T U C
E D C L W V M E N R
S D L C X A I S H Z
N Q U R E V U O Z P
X S W E A R Q A P P
G Y B U Y W H R U E
```

1. Would you please bring the coat _____ (hear, here)?

2. The children are going to the _____ (fair, fare).

3. Ken uses his _____ (write, right) hand to draw.

4. _____ (Their, There) are some cookies in the jar.

5. Linda will _____ (wear, where) a long dress for the party.

6. The kites _____ (sore, soar) high in the sky.

7. Kate will _____ (buy, by) a new watch next month.

8. Maria cut the cake into eight equal _____ (peaces, pieces)

Using Context Clues

Read the text.
Write the words in bold next to their meanings.

Suzie likes to **nurture** plants. She saw some wild plants along the street. She **wondered** how these plants are taken care of. Her mother says, " Wild plants do not **usually** need special care. These plants grow in different **habitats** such as deserts, **grasslands**, forests and seashores. Wild plants grow in different climates. Some of these plants **thrive** in hot and **humid** climates. Some plants that do not **need** much rain grow in the deserts."

require _____

normally _____

thought _____

take care of _____

land covered in

thick grass _____

the natural _____

home _____

moist _____

grow well _____

TRY IT Use any three of the words in bold in sentences of your own.

Puzzle Time!

Listed below are meanings of some words. Read the meaning and look out for the word.
Then complete the words by writing the missing letters.

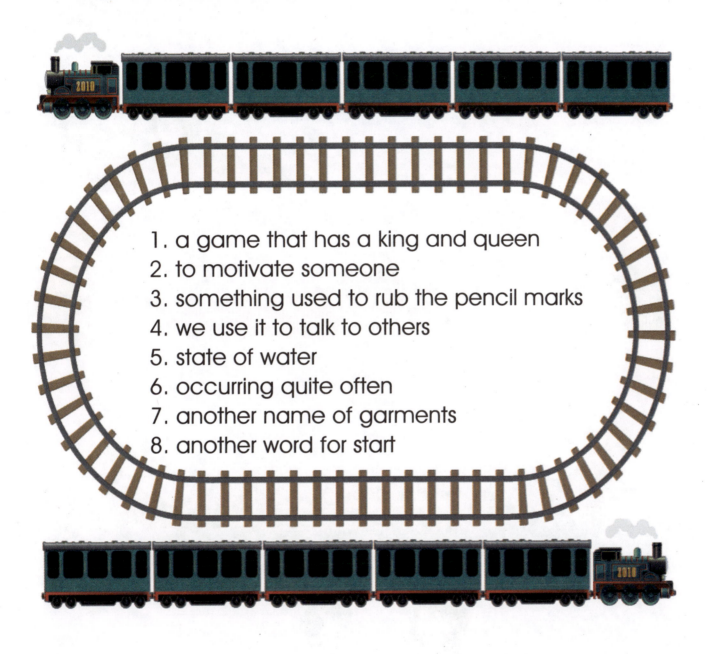

1. a game that has a king and queen
2. to motivate someone
3. something used to rub the pencil marks
4. we use it to talk to others
5. state of water
6. occurring quite often
7. another name of garments
8. another word for start

1. CH __ ___ __ __ __

2. ENCO ___ __ __ __ __

3. ER ___ ___ __ __

4. T E L E ___ __ ___ __ __

5. L I Q ___ ___ __

6. F R E Q __ __ __ __

7. C L O __ __ __ __

8. __ __ __ __ __ NING

What Does the Picture Say?

Look at the pictures. Circle the best title from among the given options.

- Benny's basket
- Benny goes on a ride

- Benny with a helmet
- Benny's house

- Sunset time
- Pogo is sad

- Off to sleep
- The Happy Pogo

- Let's sing!
- High to fly

- Rock and Roll
- Up and twist

Twist your tongue

Thirty thirsty sailors, sipping pop in pint pots
at a seaside shop
And shaking sandy seashells
on saucy seagulls!

Mama Duck and Little Duck

Look at the pictures and put a tick (✔) for the correct sentence.

1. Little Duck and Mama Duck walk along the road.
   Little Duck walks along the side of the road.

2. They are eating corns.
   They are going to the pond.

3. Little Duck and Mama Duck sit by the pond.
   Little Duck and Mama Duck walk to the field.

4. Mama Duck teaches Little Duck to swim.
   Mama Duck teaches Little Duck to cook.

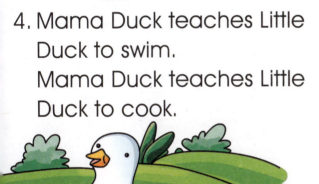

5. Little Duck swims with Mama Duck every day.
   Little Duck swims by herself now.

Maria on a Trip!

Look at the pictures.

Read these sentences and number them according to the pictures.
Write 1, 2, 3, 4 and 5.

☐ They came back home after a lot of fun.

☐ Maria's family went on a trip.

☐ They had 3 bags to carry.

☐ They also rode on a boat.

☐ Maria and her parents went to the beach.

Making Lemonade

Read how to make lemonade.

You need: some lemons, sugar, cold water, ice
1. Squeeze some lemons to make lemon juice.
2. Pour the lemon juice into a pitcher and add in some cold water.
3. Add sugar.
4. Stir and put ice.
5. Drink!

Number the pictures 1, 2, 3 and 4 to show the correct order.

Text

Read the poem. Then on each balloon, write the name of the child to which it belongs.

John's pink balloon into the sky
Can you see it fly high?
Kate's balloon, yellow and gay,
Bounced on the road far away.
Dane's balloon small and green,
Has the funniest face ever seen.
Sandy's balloon red and bright,
Has magic stars that shine at night.
Mike's balloon went hop-hop-hop
On a prickly cactus and burst POP!

Text

Read the poem.

Lima is a dog

Who wanted to change his spots.

So he bought a tin of white paint

To cover all the dots.

But no one seems to know him,

So he sits and waits for the rain,

Just hoping that a heavy shower

Will bring his spots again.

Put a tick (✓) on the correct option.

1. Who is Lima?

   a dog ☐   a leopard ☐

2. What did Lima want to hide?

   his tail ☐   his spots ☐

3. What does Lima wait for?

   snow ☐   rain ☐

4. Which other name would you like to give the poem?

   Lima's Spots ☐   White Paint ☐

Big Hat

Read the story.

Everyone called Sam – Big Hat. But why?

In winter he wore a woolen cap.

It covered his head. It came down to his shoulders too.

And it kept him very warm.

In summer, he wore a great cowboy hat.

It was wider than him. Sam had to bend sideways to get through the front door!

Fill in the blanks with words from the story.

1. Everyone called Sam

   _____

   _____,

   _____

2. He wore a

   _____

   _____ in winter.

   _____

3. Sam's summer hat was

   _____

   _____ than him.

   _____

4. His woolen hat came down to

   _____

   his _____.

   _____

Can you guess why Sam was called Big Hat? Write it here.

_____

Answer Key

Page 2

Across

1 head
4. mouth
6. ears
7. eyes
8. nose

Down

1. hair
2. bones
3. legs
5. hands.

Page 3

1. hair
2. waist
3. finger
4. neck
5. wrist
6. shoulder
7. palm
8. feet

Page 5

Words that name people are:
father, boy, girl, mother

Page 4

1. trunk
2. tentacles
3. fins
4. beak
5. shell

Page 6

a	b	c	d	e	f	g	j	h	s
i	s	o	c	k	s	j	a	k	h
l	k	m	o	n	o	p	c	q	i
r	i	p	a	n	t	s	k	s	r
t	r	u	t	v	w	x	e	y	t
z	t	a	b	c	d	e	t	f	g
h	i	j	k	l	m	n	o	p	q
t	i	e	r	s	t	h	a	t	u

Page 7

doctor	teacher	dentist
architect	fire fighter	policeman

Page 8

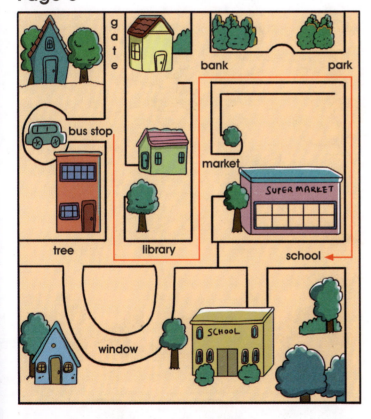

Page 11

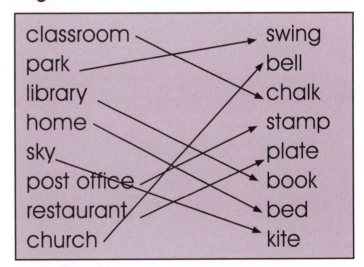

1. swing
3. stamp
5. chalk
7. bed

2. book
4. bell
6. plate
8. kite

Page 9

1. rabbit
3. ostrich
5. monkey
7. sheep
9. turtle

2. snake
4. crab
6. frog
8. mouse
10. penguin

Page 10

1. lamp
3. camera
5. pail
7. rope

2. brush
4. soap
6. clock
8. tissue

Answer Key

Page 12

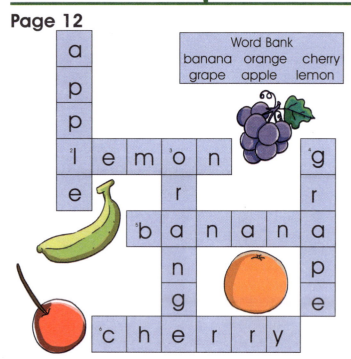

Word Bank
banana orange cherry
grape apple lemon

Page 13

1. car
2. bicycle
3. wagon
4. sleigh
5. truck
6. bus
7. airplane
8. train

Page 14

1. eraser, slides
2. lion
3. ink
4. marble
5. mittens
6. snail
7. stumps
8. socks
9. mat

Page 15

1. Hello
2. Sorry
3. Please
4. Good night
5. Excuse me

Page 16

Action words are: kick, swim, run, sleep, work, talk, sit, jump, skip, make, add

Page 17

1. play   2. cleans
3. draws   4. asks
5. gets   6. read
7. counts   8. solves

Page 18

1. weep, look, watch
2. draw, clap, write
3. mew, neigh, chirp
4. jump, walk, run
5. speak, chew, yell

Page 19

1. gallop   2. moo
3. talk   4. hop
5. squeak   6. cluck
7. crawl   8. quack

Page 20

1. hot – cold
2. sad – happy
3. day – night
4. old – new
5. big – little

Page 21

1. clean – dirty   2. near – far
3. off – on   4. noisy – quiet
5. shallow – deep   6. true – false
7. thin – thick   8. lose – win
9. soft – hard   10. open – close

Page 22

1. orange – tangy   2. honey – sweet
3. lemon – sour   4. coffee – bitter
5. chillies – spicy   6. pretzels – salty

Page 23

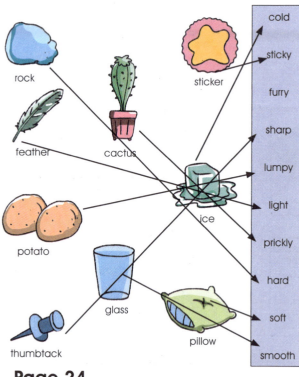

Page 24

Answer Key

Page 25
1. hairy
2. pretty
3. funny
4. wild
5. curly
6. round

Page 26
Words that rhyme are:
1. horn – corn
2. tree – bee
3. spoon – moon
4. fly – tie
5. clock – sock
6. wool – full
7. brown – down
8. pick – stick

Page 27
1. water
2. day
3.
4. feet
5. apple
6. woman
7. hand
8. vegetables

Page 28
1. pair
2. bear
3. bean
4. too
5. one
6. it
7. their
8. wait

Page 29
The answers are:
1. pencil/pen
2. shoulder
3. scissors
4. glue
5. bus
6. Monday to Friday
7. Doctor
8. Football
9. Clock
10. Chair
11. library

Page 30
1. hop, mop, pop, top
2. bench, flower, grass, tree
3. cap, jacket, shoes, trousers
4. bread, cupcake, pastry

Page 31

B	I	R	T	H	D	A	Y
J	O	L	G	I	F	T	S
F	R	O	S	T	I	N	G
K	T	L	H	A	P	P	Y
L	H	L	O	C	A	K	E
M	W	I	S	H	R	O	A
N	J	P	E	I	T	K	A
O	M	O	F	D	Y	R	V
P	I	P	C	F	E	W	D
I	C	E	C	R	E	A	M

Alphabetical order of the words:
birthday, cake, frosting , gifts, happy, ice cream, lollipop, party, wish

Page 32
Food - pasta, eggs, cornflakes, patty, cheese, toast, noodles, butter, almonds, kiwi, bread,
Drinks - milk, tea, coffee, water

Page 33

Women in the family	Places	Things you wear	Parts of your face	Size words
grandmother	market	shoes	eyebrows	short
aunt	bank	jacket	nose	tall
daughter	zoo	gloves	lips	big
mother	airport	trousers	cheeks	long

Page 34

book	rain	light
cars	magazine	sun
clock	chair	newspaper
vast	sick	squid
huge	happy	octopus
giant	healthy	drawers
sky	cookies	twelve
woods	mountain	forest
sausage	tomato	trousers

bird	goat	squirrel
grass	ladybug	orange
pillow	quilt	blanket
drill	grandma	cucumber
square	eggplant	sea
spinach	wise	sleep
lake	pond	stream
Indigo	pink	poppy
bark	branch	nest

Page 35
Odd one out in each group is:
1. secretary
2. uncle
3. smart
4. Thursday
5. tawny
6. ducklings

Page 36
1. glass, cup
2. watch, see
3. pay, buy
4. draw, paint
5. young, new
6. know, sure
7. cross, angry

Page 37
1. the ground
2. a pet
3. run
4. calf
5. a leap
6. yanking
7. a wind
8. at night

Answer Key

Page 38

1. cry
2. silent
3. warm
4. far
5. difficult
6. start
7. alone
8. true
9. quick
10. rich

hot
hard
fast
weep
correct
wealthy
quiet
begin
lonely
distant

Page 39

speak- talk
big- large
present- gift
shout- yell
loud- noisy
sweet- sugary

Page 40

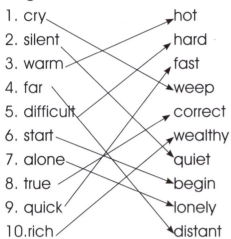

Page 41

1. quiet- noisy
2. tidiness- mess
3. loose-tight
4. shallow- deep
5. deny- accept
6. none-every
7. shrink- grow
8. polite- rude

Page 42

hide- seek
reach-leave
lose-win
repair- break
enter-exit
add- remove
strong- weak

Page 43

1. lost
2. difficult
3. never
4. dislikes
5. lost
6. sour
7. disagreed
8. common
9. foolish
10. new

Page 44

superstar
farmyard
foothill
sidewalk
eyeball
baseball
toothache
nightgown
backpack
chalkboard

Page 45

teamwork
sunset
homesick
flagpole
windshield
drumstick
scorekeeper
myself
downtown
racetrack
homework
flagstick

Page 46

1. today
2. sunshine
3. sidewalk
4. driveway
5. snowballs
6. snowman
7. something
8. seashells

Page 47

breakfast
pancakes
doorbell
sunshine
doorway
tablecloth
teapot
sunflowers

Page 49

Children will do
on their own.

Page 50

1. unwrap
2. preheat
3. return
4. unable
5. untied
6. redo
7. misspell
8. dishonest

Page 51

rewrite ✓ write again	unkind ✓ not kind	preschool ✓ before school	bicycle one-wheeled vehicle
midnight ✓ in the middle of night 12:00	dislike like very much	unsolved ✓ not solved	improper perfect
nonstop ✓ without stopping	overeat ✓ eat too much	subway ✓ under a road	replace place something again
inactive ✓ not active	exhale ✓ breathe out	invisible clearly seen	cooperate ✓ work jointly

Page 52

1. preplans
2. disorder
3. prearranges
4. unformed
5. reshapes
6. unhappy
7. rethinks
8. restarts
9. disappears
10. preview

9, 5, 6, 7
1, 4, 2, 10
8, 3

Page 54

First exercise

1. mostly
2. beautifully
3. tourist
4. coldest
5. movable
6. lately
7. driver

Second exercise

1. hopeful
2. unity
3. careless
4. weakness
5. useful
6. portable
7. beautiful
8. warmest, growing
9. droopy
10. wisdom

Answer Key

Page 55

1. rewrite
2. misread
3. careless
4. agreeable
5. kindness
6. disappear
7. misuse
8. uncovered
9. sickness
10. dishonest
11. unfair
12. helpful

Page 56

1. playful
2. useful
3. repairable
4. sadly
5. immediately
6. skilful
7. faster
8. equipment
9. brightness
10. excitement

Page 57

1. restful
2. breakable
3. comfortable
4. wearable
5. windy
6. excitement
7. leader
8. spotless
9. thoughtful
10. louder
11. colourful
12. memorable

Page 58

Across
3. density
6. courageous
8. slower
10. celebrationr

Down
1. artist
2. fearless
4. perfection
5. solvable
7. readable
9. helpful

Page 60

right-write
piece-peace
night-knight
ate-eight
which-witch

Page 61

be - bee
break - brake
I – eye
knot- not
main - mane
ate - eight
dew - due
no- know
blew- blue
hair- hare
week- weak
some- sum
roll- role
pain- pane
right- write

Page 62

1. rode
2. paws
3. passed
4. board
5. won

Children will make sentences on their own.

Page 64

Children owill do on their own.

Page 65

Children will do on their own. Answers will vary

Page 66

1. rats
2. evil, live
3. draw
4. kids
5. cafe
6. plug
7. sore

puzzle answer:
Eight ate

Page 67

school
read
leaf
run
sheep
swift
kite
master
happy

Page 68

1. play
2. enjoy
3. nice
4. love
5. end
6. try
7. build
8. cold
9. heat
10. sleep

Page 69

1. dived
2. carried
3. talked
4. washed
5. skipped
6. tried
7. planned
8. jogged
9. hurried
10. hopped

Page 70

Children will do on their own.

Page 72

a. tele
b. auto
c. cyc
d. phon
e. spher
f. bio
g. mono
h. hydro
i. therm

1. spherical
2. thermal
3. telescope
4. automobile
5. biosphere
6. symphony
7. cyclone
8. hydrant
9. monologue

Page 73

1. he's
2. who'll
3. I'm
4. haven't
5. you're
6. she'd
7. they'd
8. don't
9. let's
10. there's

Page 74

1. It's
2. We're
3. Where's
4. It's
5. I'm
6. doesn't
7. hadn't
8. They've
9. I'll
10. can't

Page 75

1. isn't
2. can't
3. they've
4. didn't
5. doesn't
6. won't
7. she'll
8. it's
9. there's
10. wouldn't

Answer Key

Page 76
1. zaps
2. zill
3. zebra
4. raze
5. zero
6. maze
7. doze
8. zoom
9. prize
10. razor
11. dozen
12. snooze

Page 77
1. l
2. h
3. k
4. l
5. l
6. k
7. g
8. b
9. h
10. b

Page 78
1. right
2. eight
3. thought
4. wrote
5. hour
6. bought
7. knitted
8. wrapped

Page 79
1. yanked
2. spotted
3. grabbed
4. dashed
5. disinfected
6. splashed
7. perfect

Page 80
1. never
2. weak
3. sour
4. deep
5. busy
6. disagree
7. common
8. slow
9. empty
10. safe

Page 81
1. here
2. fair
3. right
4. There
5. wear
6. soar
7. buy
8. pieces

Page 82
1. require- need
2. normally- usually
3. thought- wondered
4. take care of- nurture
5. land covered in thick grass- grasslands
6. the natural home- habitats
7. moist- humid
8. grow well- thrive

Page 83
1. CHESS
2. ENCOURAGE
3. ERASER
4. TELEPHONE
5. LIQUID
6. FREQUENT
7. CLOTHES
8. BEGINNING

Page 84
Children will do their own.

Page 85

1. Little Duck and Mama Duck walk along the road.

2. They are going to the pond.

3. Little Duck and Mama Duck sit by the pond.

4. Mama Duck teaches Little Duck to swim.

5. Little Duck swims by herself now.

Page 86
5   They came back home after a lot of fun.

1   Maria's family went on a trip.

2   They had 3 bags to carry.

4   They also rode on a boat.

3   Maria and her parents went to the beach.

Page 87
 1
 4
 3
 2

Page 88
Pink: John   Yellow: Kate

Green: Dane   Red: Sandy

Page 89
1. a dog
2. his spots
3. rain
4. Lima's Spots

Page 90
1. Big Hat
2. woollen cap
3. wider
4. shoulders

Because he wore a big cowboy hat.